Eye on the Universe
The Sun

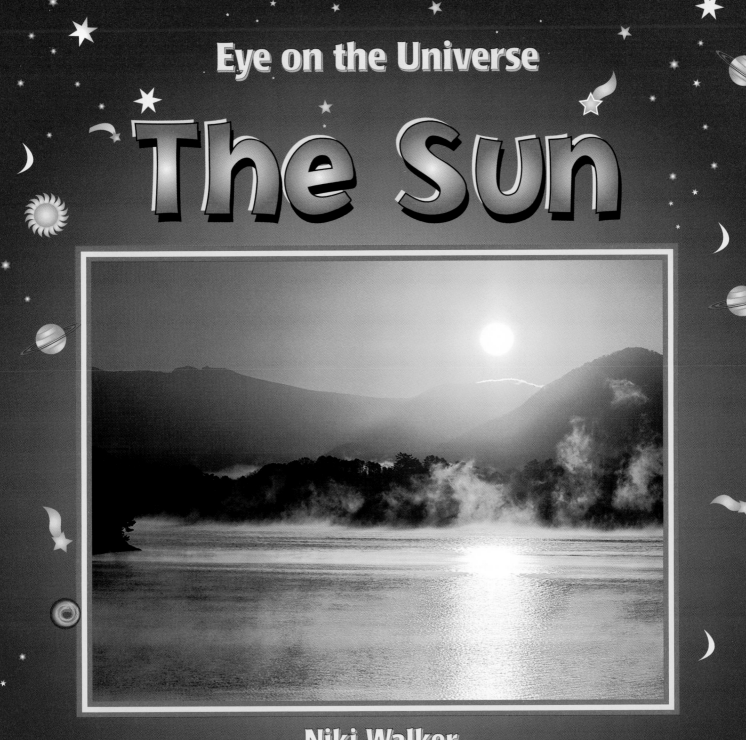

Niki Walker
Illustrated by Bonna Rouse

🌳 Crabtree Publishing Company
www.crabtreebooks.com

Eye on the Universe

Created by Bobbie Kalman

To Sigi,
with thanks for being such a good friend

Editor-in-Chief
Bobbie Kalman

Author
Niki Walker

Managing editor
Lynda Hale

Project editor
John Crossingham

Editors
Kate Calder
Hannelore Sotzek
Heather Levigne

Computer design
Lynda Hale
Niki Walker

Production coordinator
Hannelore Sotzek

Special thanks to
NASA, Dr. Hall Crannell

Consultant
Dr. Carol Jo Crannell, NASA Goddard Space Flight Center

Photographs
NASA: page 15
Other photographs by Digital Stock and Eyewire, Inc.

Illustrations and digital artwork
All illustrations by Bonna Rouse, except the following:
    Barbara Bedell: pages 18 (all except eagle), 19
    John Crossingham: pages 12 (top), 13, 17, 23, 24
    Lucy DeFazio: page 8 (bottom)

Digital prepress
Embassy Graphics

Printer
Worzalla Publishing Company

Crabtree Publishing Company

www.crabtreebooks.com   1-800-387-7650

PMB 16A
350 Fifth Avenue,
Suite 3308
New York, NY
10118

612 Welland Avenue
St. Catharines,
Ontario
Canada
L2M 5V6

73 Lime Walk
Headington,
Oxford
OX3 7AD
United Kingdom

Cataloging-in-Publication Data
Walker, Niki
    The sun

p. cm. — (Eye on the universe)
Includes index.

ISBN 0-86505-682-X (library bound) — ISBN 0-86505-692-7 (pbk.)
This book describes the characteristics of the Sun, covering such topics
as its creation and physical make-up as well as its effects on Earth.

1. Sun—Juvenile literature. [1. Sun] I. Rouse, Bonna, ill. II. Title.
III. Series: Kalman, Bobbie. Eye on the universe.

QB521.5 .W35 2001   j523.7—dc21   LC 00-060386
                                                                        CIP

Contents

What is the Sun?

It is impossible to ignore the Sun. It is the brightest object in our sky and the reason we have daylight. Every day it splashes beautiful streaks of color across the sky when it rises and sets. The Sun also warms the Earth and makes it possible for every living thing, including you, to eat, breathe, and grow. Without the Sun's light and heat, nothing could live on Earth.

Our very own star

The Sun is a **star**. Stars are huge balls of gas that glow and give off heat. The Sun is just one of billions of stars that make up our **galaxy**, the **Milky Way**. It looks different to us than the stars we see at night because it is much closer to Earth. The Sun is about 93 million miles (150 million km) away. That distance may seem far, but the next closest star, Alpha Centauri, is trillions of miles away!

Whew, that's hot!

The Sun's surface is extremely hot—about 10,000°F (5500°C). Its center is even hotter, reaching temperatures of about 27,000,000°F (15 000 000 °C). By contrast, air temperatures on Earth may reach only about 100°F (38°C) on a very hot day.

From Earth, the Sun appears to be a plain, solid disk, but up-close, its surface rolls and swirls as though it is boiling.

In Earth's sky, the Sun appears to be smaller than our planet. The Sun is about 900,000 miles (1 450 000 km) across, however. It is much bigger than Earth, which is about 7,390 miles (11 900 km) across. In fact, if the Sun were an empty container, you could put more than a million Earths inside it!

Stars

All stars are glowing balls of extremely hot gases, but they are not all the same size, temperature, and color. Our Sun, for example, is a mid-sized star with a medium temperature. Scientists call it a yellow **dwarf star**. Dwarf stars range from the smallest stars to medium-sized stars. The largest stars are called **giants**. They are up to 40 times as large as the Sun.

Star colors

Most of the stars in our night sky look like small white dots of light, but they actually come in a variety of colors, including blue, yellow, red, and orange. A star's color depends on how hot it is. Think of heated metal— it first glows red, then yellow, and finally becomes white-hot.

white dwarf

yellow dwarf

red giant

blue giant

It is easier to see the colors of the stars if you look at the night sky with a telescope or binoculars.

*1. A star begins as a nebula. Forces of **gravity** cause the nebula to be pulled together.*

A star's life

All stars go through a series of stages beginning with their birth and ending with their death. Scientists believe that stars form in clouds of dust and gas called **nebulae**. Each star begins as a small clump of dust and gas that eventually grows so large that its weight presses in on its center. The center heats up under the pressure and, in time, the gases begin to change. Hydrogen gas turns into helium and, as it changes, it releases light and heat. After billions of years have passed, the star runs out of hydrogen and dies.

2. Slowly a tight, hot ball of gas forms at the center of the nebula.

3. As the process continues, the center becomes hot enough to shine. Its temperature is now over 18,000,000 °F (10 000 000 °C)!

5. The star's gravity and heat keep it balanced, so it stays the same size. It will stay this size for about 10 billion years.

4. The nebula's remaining dust and gas spin around the new star. They may eventually join together to form planets and moons.

6. As the star runs low on hydrogen, it becomes a red giant. Its edges cool, and it swells to 500 times its original size.

7. When stars like the Sun die, they shrink and become a white dwarf. Large stars die by exploding suddenly in a **supernova**, shown here.

Our solar system

Long ago, people believed that Earth was at the center of everything in the heavens. They thought the Sun and all the other stars revolved around Earth. These beliefs were incorrect. The Sun is at the center of our **solar system**. The solar system is made up of the Sun and nine planets, as well as moons, comets, asteroids, meteoroids, and all the dust and space between them.

Pluto

Neptune

asteroid belt

Earth

Mercury

Sun

Venus

Mars

Jupiter

Saturn

Uranus

*Planets, comets, asteroids, and meteoroids **orbit**, or travel around, the Sun in **elliptical**, or oval-shaped, paths.*

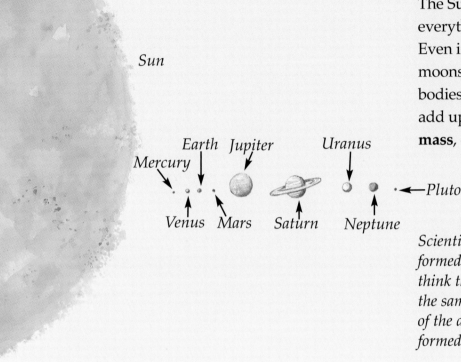

Sun

Mercury

Earth Jupiter

Uranus

Venus Mars Saturn

Neptune

←—Pluto

Big brother

The Sun is massive compared to everything else in our solar system. Even if you combined all the planets, moons, comets, asteroids, and other bodies in the solar system, they would add up to less than 1% of the Sun's **mass**, or the amount of matter inside.

Scientists believe that the solar system formed about 4.5 billion years ago. They think that everything in it formed from the same nebula. The Sun took almost all of the dust and gas. The little bit left over formed everything else in the solar system.

Innies and outies

The nine planets in our solar system are divided into two groups: the **inner planets** and the **outer planets**. The four inner planets—Mercury, Venus, Earth, and Mars—are closest to the Sun. The outer planets—Jupiter, Saturn, Uranus, and Neptune—are farther away. Pluto does not belong to either group. It is farthest from the Sun.

Around the Sun

All the planets orbit the Sun, as shown on page 8. The Sun holds the planets in their paths with its enormous gravity. Gravity is the force that pulls things toward an object. For example, when we jump, Earth's gravity pulls us back to the ground. The more material inside a star or planet and the more compact it is, the greater the gravity is on that body.

A closer look at the Sun

The Sun is so hot that no solid or liquid can exist in it, on it, or near it. It is made up entirely of gases, which means it does not have a firm surface like Earth does. The Sun is made up of several distinct layers, which are shown on the opposite page. Some layers are so hot and compressed that they look **opaque**, which means you cannot see through them.

The Sun's furnace

The center of the Sun is called the **core**. The rest of the Sun presses in on the core, so the gases there are tightly squeezed and very hot. The core's temperature is about 27,000,000°F (15 000 000°C). All of the Sun's energy comes from the core. It moves slowly outward through the layers of the Sun and then into space.

Glowing halo

A layer of gas called the **corona** surrounds the Sun. It flows into space for millions of miles, but we can see it only when the rest of the Sun is blocked, as shown right. Although the corona is far from the core, it is much hotter than the layer below it called the **photosphere**. Scientists are just beginning to understand why the corona is so hot.

prominence

corona

photosphere

core

radiation zone

convection zone

*The **chromosphere** is a thin blanket of gas that glows pink. Its name means "color sphere." It is almost impossible to see this layer because the photosphere is so much brighter.*

The surface

The photosphere is the layer of the Sun we see. It is often called the "surface," but it is not solid. This layer is made up of millions of pockets of gas called **granules**. These granules, shown right as dark spots, grow and then fade. Most granules last less than ten minutes. New granules continue to form, replacing those that have disappeared.

How the Sun makes energy

Every second, the Sun creates huge amounts of energy inside its core. From there, the energy moves slowly toward the Sun's outer edges. It can take a million years to reach space! Once it is free, the energy **radiates**, or travels in waves, away from the Sun as heat and light energy. After it leaves the Sun, the energy moves very fast. It takes about eight minutes to reach Earth. The picture on the right shows the energy's path.

Energy develops in the core. It spends about a million years inside the Sun before it is shot toward Earth.

energy

proton

neutron

electron

What is an atom?

The gases inside the Sun are made up of **atoms**. Atoms are so tiny that more than a million could fit on a pinhead! Each atom is made up of a number of smaller particles. These particles include **protons**, **neutrons**, and **electrons**. The **nucleus** is made of protons and neutrons. It is surrounded by whizzing electrons. There are 92 natural types of atoms, including carbon, oxygen, and hydrogen. An atom's type is determined by its number of protons.

What makes the Sun shine?

The Sun shines because of a chain of events called **fusion**. The pressure in the Sun's core is so strong that the hydrogen atoms are squeezed together and their electrons are stripped away. This process leaves each atom with a nucleus of one proton. An atom that is missing electrons is called an **ion**.

Under the core's heat and pressure, hydrogen ions **fuse**, or join, together and become helium. When hydrogen ions fuse into helium, a burst of energy is released. Every second, the Sun fuses millions of tons of hydrogen into helium. The huge amounts of energy that are released make the Sun glow.

hydrogen ions

energy from fusion

helium

As deuterium is formed, one ion changes and energy is released.

Under pressure

Hydrogen ions do not fuse into helium immediately. Inside the core, heat and pressure cause the ions to whip and smash into each other like cars in a giant bumper-car lot. Eventually, two hydrogen ions bump and stick together. Energy is released, and a new ion called **deuterium** is formed. Soon, another hydrogen ion sticks to the deuterium and more energy is released. This process continues until enough ions stick together to form a helium atom.

Solar activity

Like Earth, the Sun has an **equator** around its center. It also has a **north pole** and a **south pole**. An imaginary line called an **axis** extends from pole to pole through the middle of the Sun. The Sun **rotates**, or spins, on its axis. It has an unusual style of rotating, however. At the equator, the Sun makes a full rotation every 25 Earth days, but at the poles it takes 36 days. The Sun is also surrounded by a powerful **magnetic field** that curves around it from its north pole to its south pole.

Sunspots

Sunspots, shown right, are dark splotches on the surface of the Sun. They are cooler than the rest of the surface, making them appear dark. Sunspots can last from under an hour to half a year. They do not remain in one place, however. Sunspots appear to move across the surface because the Sun is always rotating. Sometimes there are almost no spots on the Sun and, at others, there more than a hundred.

Prominences

Prominences are arched streams of hot gas. This gas is **ionized**, or full of ions and electrons. The ions build up pressure, which causes the gas to erupt. The Sun's magnetic field acts as a wall and confines the streams to loops. Prominences follow the field's curve and then flow back into the photosphere.

north pole

axis

equator

south pole

inactive period

The sunspot cycle

The appearance and number of sunspots follows a regular cycle. Every eleven years, the number of sunspots increases to a very large number and then decreases again. When sunspots are at their maximum, the Sun is in an **active period**. The Sun's last active period was in 2000. During an active period, the Sun's surface also bursts in prominences and other eruptions called **flares**. Read more about active periods on page 17.

active period

The smallest sunspots are about 186 miles (300 km) across, whereas the largest are up to 62,139 miles (100 000 km) across—a size much bigger than Earth!

Flares

Flares generally erupt near sunspots. They become more common when there are many spots. Flares sometimes send huge streams of glowing gas into space and are some of the most powerful events in the solar system. They can release so much energy that they disrupt radio signals on Earth. If people could trap the energy from a single flare, it would provide enough power to supply Earth for thousands of years!

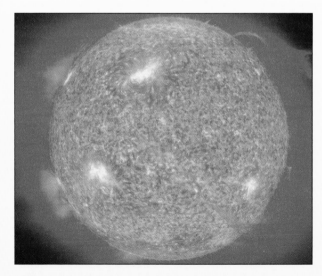

When observed with special cameras, solar flares appear as intense white patches.

Auroras

Auroras are shimmering beams of light that can be seen in the sky around Earth's North and South Poles. They are also called the **northern** and **southern lights**. Most auroras are green, red, or blue. They appear as flowing curtains, streaming arcs, or brilliant rays. They swirl, glow, and fade because streams of high-speed particles called **solar winds** hit the atmosphere in bursts.

What causes auroras?

The particles that cause auroras come from the Sun. The Sun's heat causes protons, electrons, and other ions in its outer layer to form a mixture called **plasma**. Plasma moves away from the Sun as solar wind. Earth is also surrounded by a curved magnetic field. When plasma hits this field, the particles move along it toward Earth's poles. At the poles, it crashes into the atmosphere and releases energy in bursts of colored light, or auroras.

Earth's magnetic field, shown as blue lines, shields most of the planet from solar wind plasma. When the plasma hits the field, however, it does not stop. Instead, it slides along the field until it arrives at the poles, causing auroras.

Troublemakers!

Solar winds can cause big problems on Earth. During the Sun's active periods, the winds can interfere with compasses and **satellites**. Sometimes radio and television signals become scrambled, and telephone systems experience brief problems. Solar winds can even cause power blackouts. The next time your TV screen appears fuzzy, it may be because of a strong solar wind!

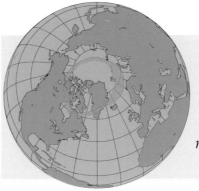

The northern lights usually appear near the Arctic, so only people living in the far north can see them.

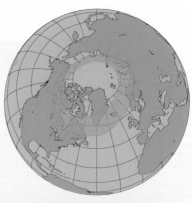

Auroras spread during an active period. The northern lights can be seen over much of North America and Europe at this time.

*Northern lights are also called the **aurora borealis**. Southern lights are the **aurora australis**. Auroras occur at both poles at the same time. They are often mirror copies of one another.*

Why we need the Sun

In addition to giving us heat and light, the Sun is also responsible for all weather patterns. Without the Sun, we would not have wind or rain.

Feeding the planet

The Sun is at the beginning of every **food chain**, such as the one shown right. Plants absorb sunlight and use it to make food. This process, called **photosynthesis**, is shown below. When an animal eats a plant, it gets the energy stored inside. When another animal eats the plant-eater, the energy moves along the food chain.

energy from the Sun

The Sun provides the energy that the strawberry plant uses to make food. Animals such as mice eat the berries. A mouse is then eaten by an eagle.

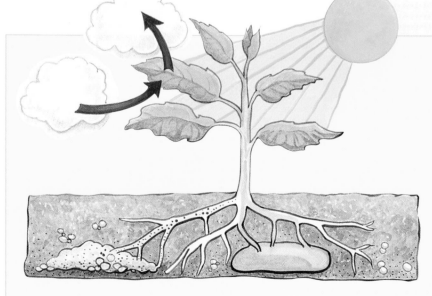

Photosynthesis turns the Sun's energy into food, which plants use to grow, survive, and reproduce. Plants combine the sunlight with water. They use some of the food they make right away and store the rest.

Weather

The Sun warms Earth's air, helping to create wind. Wind helps move rain, allowing plants and animals in different areas to get water. Wind is even an energy source, as shown by the windmills above. The Sun's heat also creates a **water cycle**, shown right. The Sun warms water from oceans and lakes, causing it to rise as **vapor**. Vapor forms clouds. When the clouds cool, the vapor **condenses** and falls back to Earth as rain or snow.

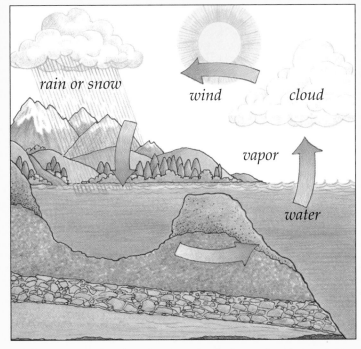

rain or snow

wind *cloud*

vapor

water

Using solar power

Every day, the Sun produces more energy than people have ever made by burning wood, coal, oil, gasoline, and other energy sources combined. **Solar power** is an important resource because it will last much longer than other energy sources and does not pollute the air and water. Many machines, from pool heaters to experimental cars, use solar energy. Some people even use a simple method of solar power to heat their home. By building a house with many windows that face the Sun, more of its heat is trapped inside the home.

Trapping the Sun

People are searching for ways to store a lot of solar energy so machines can run at night and during the winter, when there is much less sunlight. To run large machines such as cars and refrigerators you need a lot of solar power! Solar collectors for such large machines would have to be huge and take up lots of room, as shown right. Scientists are working hard to create smaller cells that can collect and store more sunlight.

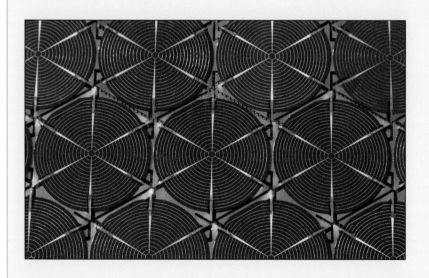

*One solar collector is made up of hundreds of **solar cells**. This photograph shows a close-up view of solar cells. A small group of cells can collect enough energy to run small machines such as calculators.*

Solar panels

Many buildings use **solar panels** to create heat and hot water. The panels are mounted on the outside of a building, so the panel's black lining can absorb the Sun's heat. The heat warms cold water flowing through a pipe inside the panel, and the water then flows out of the solar panel to be used in the building.

foil

black liner

glass

copper pipe

hot water

cold water

Time and seasons

Earth is in constant motion. It orbits the Sun and, while it travels, rotates on its axis. As Earth rotates, we experience day or night, depending on which side of the planet faces the Sun. As it orbits the Sun, we experience different seasons. It takes Earth a year to make one full trip around the Sun and begin the cycle of seasons again. Long ago, people realized that the Sun follows recognizable patterns throughout the day and through the seasons. They used these patterns to keep track of time.

This picture of northern Alaska looks like morning, but it is really midnight! During summer in the far north, that part of Earth is tilted on its axis toward the Sun. As a result, the Sun never sets in summer.

Sundials

Many years ago, people figured out that they could use a shadow to tell time, so they designed the **sundial**. As the Sun moves through the sky, its rays shine on the sundial from different angles, causing the shadow to fall on different areas on the sundial. Where the shadow falls on a sundial shows the time.

This sundial shows the shadow at noon.

This sundial shows the shadow on the three o'clock line.

Changing seasons

Earth tilts on its axis as it orbits the Sun. As Earth moves around the Sun, its northern half, or **hemisphere**, receives more or less sunlight than the southern one. These changes in sunlight create different seasons. When the northern hemisphere is tipped toward the Sun, it is summer in that part of the world. The Sun's rays hit the hemisphere almost directly, so days are warm and bright.

A day also lasts longer in summer than in winter. When the northern hemisphere is tilted away from the Sun, it is winter. The Sun's rays hit the hemisphere at an angle, so they are not as strong as in summer. Days are cooler and dimmer as a result. In spring and autumn, both hemispheres get almost the same amount of sunlight, so temperatures are milder in both parts of the world.

North American seasons

Near Earth's equator, the Sun is never far from directly overhead at noon. Temperatures stay warm all year at the equator because the Sun's rays always hit it almost directly.

axis

autumn

When it is winter in the north, it is summer in the southern hemisphere.

winter

equator

summer

spring

*Earth has two **solstices** a year. They occur when the Sun reaches its farthest distance north or south of the equator. Winter solstice is the year's shortest day, and summer solstice is the longest day.*

*Earth also has two **equinoxes**, or days when there are equal amounts of daylight and darkness. These occur on the first day of spring, and on the first day of autumn.*

Eclipses

People may not always notice it, but there is a lot of movement happening in space. As Earth travels around the Sun, the Moon travels around the moving Earth. Sometimes as these bodies make their orbit, their paths cross. Once in a while, the Moon comes between Earth and the Sun and blocks the Sun from our view. This event is called a **solar eclipse**. Remember that it is never safe to look at the Sun, even when it is blocked by the Moon! To watch an eclipse safely, make the observatory described on page 31.

*There are three types of solar eclipses. A **total eclipse** occurs when the Moon blocks the Sun completely. Only the corona is visible.*

*You can still see the Sun's photosphere during an **annular eclipse**. Annular means "ring."*

Partial eclipses occur when the Moon is only partially in line with Earth and the Sun.

Blocking the Sun

The Sun is 400 times larger than the Moon, so how can the Moon hide the Sun from our view? At certain times in its orbit, the Moon is exactly 400 times closer to Earth than the Sun is, so the Moon and the Sun appear to be the same size in our sky. When the Moon is farther away, it cannot block the Sun completely, so we see an annular eclipse.

Umbra—the Moon blocks all of the Sun's rays.

Penumbra—the Moon is not fully in front of the Sun, so only some rays are blocked.

The area on Earth in line with the umbra sees a total eclipse. The areas in the penumbra see a partial eclipse.

*Just before the Sun is completely blocked during a total eclipse, a round glare sometimes peaks around the Moon. This light is called a **diamond ring effect** because it looks like a jewel in the sky.*

Bending sunlight

Sunlight looks white, but it is actually a combination of all seven colors of light. We can see these colors, called the **spectrum**, only when they are split apart. Sunlight splits when it is bent, or **refracted**, as it passes through different substances, such as air, water, or glass. Sunlight refracts when it travels from one material into another because the new substance causes it either to speed up or slow down. Refraction occurs where the two materials meet. This area is called the **interface**.

sunlight

spectrum

Colors of the rainbow

A rainbow forms when sunlight passes through water droplets in the air. The droplets bend, split, and reflect the sunlight. The raindrops are natural **prisms**.

Prisms

Light can be split with a triangular piece of glass called a prism.

1. Light bends as it passes through the first side because the glass slows it down.

2. The colors move through the glass at different speeds, causing them to separate. Red moves fastest, and violet is slowest.

3. The beams refract once more as they leave the prism.

Have you ever noticed that the colors of a rainbow are always the same—red, orange, yellow, green, blue, indigo, and violet? They always appear in the same order, too.

Sunny skies

Earth is surrounded by a layer of air called the **atmosphere**. The air in the atmosphere gets thicker closer to Earth. When sunlight from space reaches the atmosphere, it slows down and bends just as it does when it passes from air into glass. The way the light travels through the atmosphere affects how the Sun and the sky appear to us.

Sunsets are red and orange because blue and yellow light from the sun are absorbed by dust in the atmosphere.

Why a blue sky?

Sunlight gets scattered by dust and air particles in the atmosphere. Blue, indigo, and violet light are affected more than the other colors. They get scattered around the atmosphere, so the sky appears blue to us. The violet and indigo light is almost impossible for our eyes to see. Scientists study the sky with sophisticated instruments to see bands of violet and indigo.

When the Sun is setting, its light must travel through more atmosphere before we can see it than when it is directly above us. The long red and orange rays are the only rays that can reach Earth's surface as the Sun dips below the horizon.

atmosphere

The fan-shaped beams of light that shoot out from the Sun are called **crepuscular rays**. They are created when sunlight filters through clouds in the sky.

Fun with the Sun!

Make a "sunset"

You need a clear glass or bowl filled with water, milk, a spoon, and a flashlight.

Place your glass of water on a table and shine the flashlight through it. Look at it from the opposite side. Add spoonfuls of milk to the water. Stop when the water is cloudy and you cannot see through it. What do you see when you look at the flashlight through the milky water? The milk in the water acts like the dust in the atmosphere, which scatters light and causes red sunsets.

Make a rainbow

You need a garden hose with a "spray" nozzle (ask permission to use it!) and a sunny day.

Stand outside with the Sun to your back, as shown above. Aim the hose into the air, and spray a fine mist of water upward. What do you see? What happens if you try spraying the water when facing the Sun? Why do you think this happens? (turn back to page 26 for a reminder)

Make a sun observatory

To be able to look at the Sun, you must project it onto another surface. You can use this homemade observatory to find sunspots or watch eclipses. You need a piece of cardboard, a hole punch, tape, a wooden stake, a mirror, and white paper.

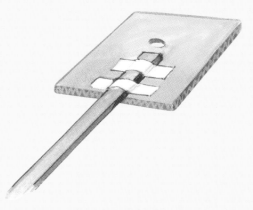

1. Punch a hole in the cardboard and tape it to the wooden stake.

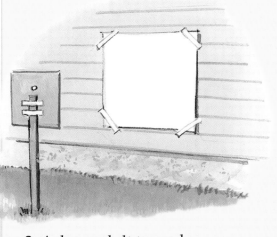

2. Ask an adult to push the stake into the ground a few feet from a wall. Tape the paper to the wall directly in front of the cardboard.

3. Ask the adult to hold the mirror behind the hole in the cardboard, so that the mirror reflects sunlight through the hole. Do you see the Sun on the paper? Are there any dark spots? Trace them on the paper and repeat the experiment in a few days. Have the spots moved?

Glossary

electron A tiny negatively charged atomic particle

equinox One of two days every year when day and night are of equal length

flare An eruption of gas from the Sun's surface

fusion The joining of two atoms into a larger atom

galaxy A massive grouping of millions of stars

gravity The force that pulls objects toward the center of a star, planet, or moon

ion An atom that has lost one or more electrons

nebula A giant cloud of dust and gas in space

neutron A tiny atomic particle with no charge

nucleus A group of protons and neutrons found at the center of an atom

orbit (n) The path taken by a satellite in space; (v) To travel around a planet or star

penumbra The outer part of the Moon's shadow cast during a solar eclipse

plasma A mixture of particles, made of ions, protons, and electrons, formed on the outer layers of the Sun

prism A solid transparent object, usually glass, that splits light that passes through it into a spectrum

proton A tiny positively charged atomic particle

satellite A natural or artificial object that travels around a star, planet, or moon

solar wind A high-speed stream of plasma ejected from the Sun's surface

solstice One of two days every year when the Sun appears to be at its maximum distance north or south of Earth's equator

supernova An enormous and sudden explosion that occurs at the end of a giant star's life

umbra The dark, central part of the Moon's shadow cast during a solar eclipse

Index

1 2 3 4 5 6 7 8 9 0   Printed in the U.S.A.   9 8 7 6 5 4 3 2 1 0